[IRIS]

[IRIS]

THEODORE JAMES, JR.

PHOTOGRAPHS BY HARRY HARALAMBOU

HARRY N. ABRAMS, INC., PUBLISHERS

For our dear friend Chris Gismondi

EDITOR: Sharon AvRutick
DESIGNER: Helene Silverman
PRODUCTION MANAGER: Maria Pia Gramaglia

Library of Congress Cataloging-in-Publication Data

James, Theodore.
  Iris / Theodore James, Jr. ; photographs by Harry Haralambou.
    p. cm.
Includes bibliographical references and index.
  ISBN 0-8109-9150-0 (pbk. with flaps)
  1. Irises (Plants) I. Haralambou, Harry. II. Title.

SB413.I8 J36 2003
635.9'3438--dc21

                    2002152587

Printed and bound in China

10 9 8 7 6 5 4 3 2 1

Harry N. Abrams, Inc.
100 Fifth Avenue
New York, N.Y. 10011
www.abramsbooks.com

Abrams is a subsidiary of
 LA MARTINIÈRE
            GROUPE

ACKNOWLEDGMENTS
We are grateful for the kind assistance and advice that was graciously given by so many
of the members of the American Iris Society, as well as those who offer plants by mail
order. Rita Gormley of Gormley Greenery was especially helpful in sharing plant
material as well as information on the growing of various iris varieties. Jim Hedgecock of
Comanche Acres Iris Gardens very kindly gave us permission to use some photographs of
Spuria and Louisiana irises (pages 41 top, 42, 43 bottom). White Flower Farm, Carol
Draycott of Draycott Gardens, Liz Schreiner of Schreiner's Iris Gardens, Kim Khlem of
Khlem's Songsparrow Perennial Farm, Gloria McMillen of McMillen's Iris Garden, Steve
Jones of Fieldstone Gardens, and Greg McCullough of Iris City Gardens all were very kind
in providing us with plant material, advice, and information.

PAGE 1: WHITE-AND-PURPLE BEARDED IRISES COMBINE WONDERFULLY WITH APRICOT PANSIES.
PAGE 2: A DRAMATIC MASS PLANTING OF SIBERIAN IRISES. PAGE 7: JAPANESE IRISES. PAGES 8–9:
AN ARRAY OF TALL BEARDED IRISES: DARKER-COLORED IRISES SUCH AS 'COUNTRY CHARM'
(ABOVE RIGHT) RETAIN THEIR RICHNESS IN BRIGHT SUNLIGHT.

CONTENTS

Anatomy of the Bearded Iris

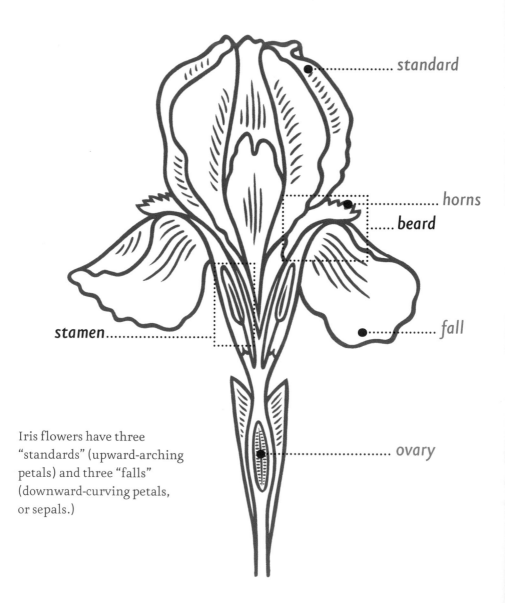

standard

horns

beard

stamen

fall

Iris flowers have three "standards" (upward-arching petals) and three "falls" (downward-curving petals, or sepals.)

ovary

THE GENUS *IRIS* INCLUDES AT LEAST 200 SPECIES, SEPARATED INTO TWO MAJOR GROUPS, RHIZOMATOUS AND BULBOUS. RHIZOMES ARE HORIZONTALLY GROWING UNDERGROUND STEMS THAT ARE USED AS FOOD STORAGE FOR THE PLANT; BEARDED, SIBERIAN, AND JAPANESE IRISES FALL INTO THIS GROUP. BULBOUS IRISES FORM A MORE TYPICAL BULB AND INCLUDE THE DUTCH IRIS, *I. DANFORDIAE*, AND *I. RETICULATA*.

ILLUSTRATION: MEGAN MONTAGUE CASH

INTRODUCTION

THE ROSE IS often called "the Queen of the Garden." If that's true, then certainly the iris must be king. Second in popularity in the United States and Great Britain only to the rose, irises are among the most beloved of all garden plants. They are infinitely easier to grow and maintain than the lovely rose, and will usually bloom gloriously even if benignly neglected. Their fragrance is hauntingly sensual, their colors and shapes are stunningly beautiful, and—to make them even more appealing to gardeners everywhere—they are among the most disease- and pest-free plants available. Irises are not fussy about soil, requiring only good drainage, they endure summer drought, and they multiply freely but are not an invasive nuisance plant. They offer almost instant gratification in that they usually bloom the year after being planted. And perhaps most importantly, they provide nothing short of one of the greatest garden spectacles of all.

They are the near-perfect plant for today's busy gardener.

SOME IRIS TERMINOLOGY

BICOLOR: lighter-colored standards; falls of a deeper contrasting color
BITONE: two shades of the same color; falls are usually darker
PLICATA: stitched margins of color on the rims of the petals,
SIGNALS: different color spots on the falls just below the beard

THERE IS NOTHING MORE LOVELY THAN THE NEWLY OPENED PETALS OF AN IRIS. HERE TALL BEARDED 'BEVERLY SILLS' IS GETTING READY TO SING.

1 Irises in History

IN THE HISTORY of the iris, which dates back to antiquity, the flower has always been associated with royalty. Records reveal that the earliest iris ever grown may be dated back to 7000 BC. The unmistakable blossoms appear in hieroglyphics carved in ancient Egyptian tombs and monuments and are listed there as medicinal plants. Between three and four thousand years ago, on one of the walls of the Palace of Knossos on Crete (the home of the Minoan civilization), a stucco relief was created that shows a Minoan prince or king wandering idyllically through a vast field of waist-high irises. In the Middle East, several centuries later, the Persian Empire's documents on the agriculture of the area suggest that the farmers collected local iris species.

A comparatively short time after irises bloomed on Minoan walls, they appeared sculpted in stone at Karnak in Egypt. Thutmose III (1504–1450 BC) celebrated the conquest of a large slice of Asia Minor by having a garden built near one of his palaces to display some of the plants—including irises—that he had brought back from his campaign. He thought irises exotic enough to be carved into stone on the great wall of the temple of Anon. The representations are unmistakable.

These captivating flowers are named after Iris, the Greek goddess of the rainbow. She was the messenger for Hera, the queen of the goddesses, and the Greeks believed that she brought Hera's messages to earth via the rainbow, an ancient Greek symbol of hope. Another of Iris' duties was to guide the souls of deceased women to the paradise of the Elysian Fields, and thus it was traditional in ancient Greece to plant purple irises on women's graves.

The ancients left word of her for all to read today. She is a significant character, the messenger of Zeus, in *The Iliad*, in which her devotion to other gods and goddesses—particularly to Aphrodite, the goddess of beauty—is documented.

IRIS BUCHARICA, NATIVE TO CENTRAL ASIA, HAS INTERESTING FOLIAGE AS WELL AS BEAUTIFUL FLOWERS. IT WILL DO WELL IN A WARM AND SHELTERED AREA OF YOUR GARDEN.

The Greek philosopher Theophrastus is credited with what is probably the first description of irises being used in perfume. It is the earliest reference we have to orrisroot—a powder derived from the rhizomes of certain Bearded iris species—which is still used today as a fixative for flower oils in potpourri and perfumes. While the Egyptians cultivated irises, both the Greeks and the Romans used the rhizomes for medicinal purposes and in perfumery.

The next major reference we have to irises is in the work of Dioscorides, who wrote of their medical uses in his Vienna Codex. Beyond scenting, the iris was thought to remove freckles, heal ulcers, and induce sleep. Pliny the Elder wrote of iris cultivation and noted that the choicest varieties came from Silistria (now Romania) and Pamphylia (now Turkey). Since its scent is sweet and cleansing, the Romans used orrisroot to freshen their breath and to add subtle flavor to their wines. After the fall of Rome, Early Christians had rosary beads carved out of the lovely scented orrisroot to wear around their necks.

During the Dark Ages and on into the Middle Ages, the iris became the symbolic signature of France and became known as the fleur-de-lis. We do not know whether the word *lis* derives from "Lys," a Flemish river, "Louis," the name of a king, or "luce," which means light. The image is that of *Iris pseudacorus* (Yellow Flag), which is to this day a common flower in boggy areas of Europe and is still used extensively in water gardens throughout the world.

There are several legends offered as explanation of the iris' long association with France. One is that during a twelfth-century battle, King Louis VII was trying to escape his enemies by crossing the river Lys when he spotted an area where clumps of *Iris pseudacorus* were growing. Louis knew this meant that the water in that area must be shallow, so he and his army were able to make a successful getaway. Afterward, he picked one of the flowers and held it up; it became a symbol of French survival. Other tales tell other stories; in any event, the fleur-de-lis became the symbol of France for the next twelve hundred years, until the revolution.

THE STRONG PINK OF THE ASTILBE IN THIS PLANTING SEEMS TO INTENSIFY THE BLUE OF THE SIBERIAN IRIS.

Irises were grown in the palaces and gardens of Moorish Spain: at the Alhambra in Granada and the Alcazar in Seville. In the area around Florence, rhizomes were planted, and three years later, harvested, skinned, dried in the sun, and used in the perfume industry. In 1876 alone, about ten thousand tons of iris rhizomes were exported from Florence to markets all over the world. In Germany, orrisroot was put in beer barrels to help keep the beer fresh. In France, it was hung in wine casks to enhance the bouquet of the wine. The English used it to flavor brandy, and the Russians used it in a popular soft drink that was made with honey and ginger.

In Japan ladies used the powder made from orrisroot to whiten their faces; rhizomes of *Iris tectorum* produced a similar powder used for that purpose. And Native Americans as well as Europeans used the fibers from the leaves of several varieties of irises to make rope.

The lovely iris has long been used in art and as an inspiration for decorative motifs. Perhaps the earliest depiction is in *Adorazione* by the Flemish painter of the Northern Renaissance Hugo van der Goes (1435–82). Both *Iris florentina* and *Iris germanica* (the popular Bearded iris) are represented. Leonardo da Vinci included irises in the *Madonna of the Rocks*. They are depicted in ancient Japanese and Persian art and in India; representations of *Iris susiana* are carved into the stone of the Taj Mahal.

Irises remain a very popular and recurring motif. In 1988, at the Glasgow Garden Festival in Scotland, three giant steel irises were used as street architecture and became the symbol of the festival. And to this day, the city emblem of New Orleans, true to its French origins, is the fleur-de-lis.

ALICE LEVIEN OF CUTCHOGUE, LONG ISLAND, CREATED A BOGGY ENVIRONMENT FOR THIS PLANTING OF YELLOW FLAG IRISES. ABOVE IT, COTONEASTER CASCADES OVER A RETAINING WALL AND GIVES INTEREST THROUGHOUT THE SEASON. OVERLEAF: THIS STUNNING SPECIMEN OF A JAPANESE IRIS SHOWS OFF ITS PURPLE AND YELLOW ATTIRE. BREATHTAKING, ISN'T IT?

2 Selecting Irises

THERE IS SO much to choose from in the wonderful world of irises. Regardless of time, money, or space limitations, there is an iris for every conceivable kind of gardening situation. There are many classifications of irises, but we'll focus on Bearded, Beardless, and Bulbous. Iris flowers come in blue, brown, pink, purple, white, and yellow—in fact, in every color of the rainbow. They also come in color combinations and pattern varieties. The foliage is spear-like, semi-evergreen, and grows in fan-shaped clumps. There have always been a few irises that surprise with a second bloom in late summer or early fall, but hybridizers have been developing new varieties of "rebloomers," which have become very popular in the past few years.

BEARDED IRISES

Bearded irises are among the easiest perennials to grow. They thrive from Canada to the Deep South. Minimal attention should result in stunning displays every spring.

The name "bearded" derives from the presence of a soft, fuzzy strip on each of the three drooping sepals, called "falls." The botanically true petals that stand upright are called "standards." All Bearded iris varieties bloom in the spring, from April to June, depending on the cultivars.

Bearded irises have thick, fleshy, underground stems called rhizomes that store food produced by the leaves. Each year underground offsets, or side shoots, develop from the original rhizome. Buds produce a large fan of leaves and several flower stalks. Success with Bearded irises depends on keeping the rhizomes firm and healthy. In general, the best approach is to provide them with good drainage while keeping the feeder roots below moist but not wet.

The American Iris Society has designated different categories of irises within the Bearded group, based on stem height and season of bloom. For

ALTERNATING SIBERIAN IRISES AND *ALCHEMILLA MOLLIS* (LADY'S MANTLE) PRODUCE A WONDERFUL BLUE-AND-YELLOW EFFECT ALONG A GARDEN PATH.

the sake of convenience and to avoid errors, they are often referred to by abbreviations: Miniature Dwarf Bearded (MDB), Standard Dwarf Bearded (SDB), Intermediate Bearded (IB), Miniature Tall Bearded (MTB), Border Bearded (BB), and Tall Bearded (TB). The four classes in the middle are known collectively as Medians.

MINIATURE DWARF BEARDED IRISES (MDB)

These are the tiniest of the Bearded irises and the earliest to bloom. They are perfect for use in rock gardens, containers, and troughs, along with tiny alpine plants; or use them at the front of borders to produce an early spring splash of color. They grow only 4–10 inches high with 1–3-inch flowers.

There are scores of varieties of Miniature Dwarf irises. Some recommended and readily available varieties are:

VARIETY	DESCRIPTION
'Alpine Lake'	White-tipped blue with blue falls
'Bantam'	Wine-purple
'Betwixt'	Light violet with purple spot
'Broad Grin'	Pale amber-pink
'Bugsy'	Yellow with black-and-yellow falls
'Ditto'	Cream and maroon bicolor
'Gnuz Spread'	Yellow
'Inner Fires'	Orange with brown falls
'Libation'	Wine-red with yellow beards
'Sleepy Time'	Light blue with white beards
'Snowy River'	Pure white
'Zipper'	Yellow with medium blue beards
REBLOOMER	
'Ditto'	Cream and maroon bicolor

Miniature Dwarf Bearded irises (above: 'Sarah Taylor'; below right: 'Joe Cool') come in a wide range of colors and work well with other plants. Below left: Intermediate Bearded iris 'Hot Spice' has its turn after the Dwarfs' show is over.

ABOVE: STANDARD DWARF BEARDED IRISES ('SLEEPY TIME') NEAR THE WATER GARDEN, AMONG BRIGHT-YELLOW HOSTA AND PHLOX. BELOW: STANDARD DWARF AND MINIATURE DWARF BEARDED IRISES ARE GROUPED WITH BRIGHT RED ANEMONES, ADDING A SPLASH OF COLOR TO THE ROCK GARDEN.

STANDARD DWARF BEARDED IRISES (SDB)

These bloom just after the Miniature Dwarfs in early spring, and range in height from 8 to 15 inches with flowers that are 2–4 inches wide. They are ideal plants for edgings at the front of borders, as well as in alpine gardens. Unlike most of their sisters, they bloom well in shady areas. Most varieties form good sturdy clumps of spike-like leaves, which eventually grow into a cushion shape. Because they are low growing, blooms are observed from above rather than from the side. The falls stand out horizontally from the standards, making for an especially colorful display. Since they bloom very early, during the dreary days of late winter and early spring, they can be best appreciated in dooryard gardens, or along paths where you walk regularly. Pests and diseases rarely attack them.

There are several hundred varieties of Standard Dwarf Bearded irises. Here are some of the most readily available recommended varieties.

VARIETY	DESCRIPTION
'Bay Ruffles'	Ruffled; light blue
'Bedford Lilac'	Flax blue with blue spot
'Chances'	Coral apricot with white spot
'Chubby Cheeks'	Ruffled; violet plicata on white
'Gemstar'	Deep violet-blue with white beards
'Ice and Indigo Blue'	White with dark blue-violet fall spot
'Jazzamatazz'	Ruffled; cream-lemon with ruby spot
'Minidragon'	Deep red bitone with orange beard
'Pele'	Orange with deep rose fall spot
'Serenity Prayer'	Cream-white with deep-blue beards
'Violet Lulu'	Soft violet
REBLOOMERS	
'Baby Blessed'	Light yellow
'Darling'	Purple
'Jewel Baby'	Deep purple
'Little Showoff'	White with blue beard
'Plum Wine'	Plum red with violet shading
'Refined'	Pale yellow
'Sun Doll'	Yellow

Intermediate Bearded Irises (IB)

Boasting upright, tall plants (16–28 inches high) with blossoms near the tops of the stalks, Intermediate Bearded irises bloom after the Dwarfs and before the Tall Bearded irises. Use them in tandem with late-flowering tulips for a special touch in your garden. Vigorous growers, they are halfway in height between the Standard Dwarf and the Tall Bearded irises, resist pests and disease, and work very well with perennials in mixed beds and borders. Their height makes them ideal for growing in the middle of a bed or border. And they usually do not need staking, because their stalks are thick and sturdy.

Here are some of the more readily available recommended varieties.

VARIETY	DESCRIPTION
'Ask Alma'	Shrimp pink
'Baby Blue Marine'	Pale blue
'Blue-Eyed Blond'	Yellow; true-blue beards
'Cee Jay'	Violet and white
'Honey Glazed'	Cream and caramel
'Lemon Pop'	Lemon yellow
'Maui Moonlight'	Ruffled; soft yellow
'Protocol'	Brilliant yellow
'Rare Edition'	White-banded violet
'Red Zinger'	Red with dark red spot
REBLOOMERS	
'Blessed Again'	Light yellow
'I Bless'	Cream; flowers nearly all summer
'Low Ho Silver'	Silvery white
'Precious Little Pink'	Pale pink

A WELL-BALANCED COMBINATION OF RUST-COLORED INTERMEDIATE BEARDED IRISES 'HOT SPICE,' LIME-GREEN HOSTA, YELLOW *LAMIUM*, AND PALE-PINK *GERANIUM SANQUINEUM*.

Miniature Tall Bearded Irises (MTB)

Known also as Table irises, these grow 16–25 inches tall, with 2–3½-inch flowers. They bloom at the same time as Border Bearded irises, but because their flowers are smaller, they are somewhat more graceful. They make excellent cut flowers for arrangements, because they combine well with and do not overpower other flowers. In the garden their flowers stand well above the leaves, so they are effective in borders and beds.

The following varieties are readily available and recommended.

VARIETY	DESCRIPTION
'Apricot Drops'	Apricot
'Bumblebee Delight'	Gold with brick red
'Chickee'	Burnished gold
'Disco Jewel'	Copper, henna, brown
'Frosted Velvet'	White with purple falls
'In Fashion'	Deep violet, white beard
'Jolly Jim'	White with orange beard
'Petite Monet'	True blue
'Rosemary's Dream'	Old rose on cream

Miniature Tall Bearded irises do not rebloom.

MAGNIFICENT TALL BEARDED IRISES COME IN ENDLESS COLORS AND COMBINE WELL WITH OTHER PLANTS IN MYRIAD WAYS. OPPOSITE: 'TEMPLE GOLD'; ABOVE: 'MOON JOURNEY'; BELOW: 'BEVERLY SILLS.'

BORDER BEARDED IRISES (BB)

These Bearded irises, which grow to a height of 16–27 inches, are smaller versions of the Tall Bearded irises, usually flowering just before them. They have short, sturdy stems so are very well suited to windy areas; they can endure heavy downpours. They do well in smaller gardens, where they do not overwhelm the other plantings. Border Bearded irises start to flower as soon as the Intermediate Bearded irises end.

Here are some readily available recommended varieties:

VARIETY	DESCRIPTION
'Baboon Bottom'	Pink-streaked cream and silver
'Brown Lasso'	Gold with lavender-and-brown falls
'Calico Kid'	Pink with purple splashes
'Cranapple'	Cranapple red
'Lyrique'	Silvery blue-violet with plum spot
'Maui Magic'	Violet; satin sheen
'Pink Bubbles'	Laced, rich pink
'Sunspinner'	Bright yellow blended into white
'Tulare'	Yellow with orange beards
REBLOOMERS	
'Double Up'	Blue-and-white bicolor with dark violet borders
'Ultra Echo'	Lavender with violet

OVERLEAF, LEFT: THIS TALL BEARDED IRIS HAS STUNNING RUFFLED PETALS THAT GIVE THE APPEARANCE OF TEXTURE. YELLOW LUPINES WOULD COMPLEMENT IT BEAUTIFULLY. OVERLEAF, RIGHT: AFTER A HEAVY RAIN, THE LOW BRANCHES OF OUR KOUSA DOGWOOD BENT OVER ENOUGH TO PARTIALLY COVER THIS TALL BEARDED IRIS. WE DIDN'T PLAN THIS; ALL WE COULD DO WAS MARVEL AT NATURE'S WORK.

Tall Bearded Irises (TB)

And finally, we have the magnificent Tall Bearded irises with their flamboyant 6–7-inch blooms on stems 30–40 inches and taller. They carry as many as twelve buds on every stem and are the last of the Bearded to bloom in the garden, usually in late spring or early summer. They are also known as Purple Flag or German irises (*Iris germanica*).

Some of the favorite Tall Bearded irises of members of the American Iris Society:

VARIETY	DESCRIPTION
'Before the Storm'	Near black
'Beverly Sills'	Pink
'Conjuration'	White and violet with white horns
'Dusky Challenger'	Dark purple
'Edith Wolford'	Yellow standards; blue-violet falls
'Hello Darkness'	Purple black
'Honky Tonk Blues'	Hyacinth blue
'Jesse's Song'	White-and-violet plicata
'Lady Friend'	Garnet
'Silverado'	Light silver-blue
'Stairway to Heaven'	Off-white standards; medium-blue falls
'Stepping Out'	White-and-violet plicata
'Thornbird'	Ecru, tan, violet with horns
'Titan's Glory'	Dark violet
'Vanity'	Pink
REBLOOMERS	
'Belvi Queen'	Cinnamon and white
'Clarence'	White with violet falls
'Eternal Bliss'	Violet with tangerine falls
'Feed Back'	Medium blue-violet
'Immortality'	White; ruffled
'Pink Attraction'	Ruffled; pale pink
'Queen Dorothy'	White with lavender stitching and old styling

BEARDLESS IRISES

Another large group of rhizomatous irises are the Beardless varieties. The most conspicuous difference between these and the Bearded are that—not surprisingly—there are no beards on the falls of the flowers. While there are hundreds of esoteric Beardless varieties, the most popular and best known are the Siberians, Japanese, Spurias, and Louisianas.

Siberian Irises (SIB)

Siberian irises are the workhorse perennial of the garden. And what a blessing they are! They're rugged, easy to grow, pest and disease free, and drought resistant. They thrive on neglect, multiply readily, adapt to all climates, and have tall, elegant foliage, gorgeous, delicate long-stem flowers, and attractive seed pods. What more could any gardener ask? Siberian irises bloom from late spring to early summer, sometimes reblooming from mid-summer to fall. They grow in clumps 1–4 feet tall and 1–3 feet wide with bloom colors in variations of white, blue, purple, yellow, and maroon.

In March, April, May, June, and throughout the summer and fall, as I wander through my garden, enjoying each and every spectacle I have created, none gives me more pleasure than my plantings of Siberian irises. Through the years I have acquired about a dozen different varieties.

The following varieties are recommended and readily available.

VARIETY	DESCRIPTION
'Caesar's Brother'	Dark violet with white signals
'Coronation Anthem'	Mid-deep blue; large cream signals
'Esther C.D.M.'	Pure white
'High Standards'	Tall; dark purple
'Indy'	Flaring red-violet
'Jeweled Crown'	Deep wine-red; gold blaze
'Mesa Pearl'	Pale lavender
'Orville Fay'	All blue
'Roaring Jelly'	Dappled bright raspberry
'Strawberry Fair'	Ruffled; strawberry-pink

Colorful and easy to grow, Siberian irises are the answer to many gardeners' dreams. Below: Blue and purple Siberian irises growing in a nursery.

The tendency of some Siberian irises to extend their bloom season—sometimes as an apparently continuous long season, other times in two distinct blooming spurts—is called "repeat bloom" to distinguish it from the Bearded irises that have two clearly separated bloom seasons, called "rebloom." Repeat bloom tends to occur on divisions at least two years old. These are the Siberians reported to exhibit repeat bloom most reliably:

VARIETY	DESCRIPTION
'Lavender Light'	Lavender with small white blaze
'My Love'	Azure blue
'Reprise'	Medium violet with dark veins
'Soft Blue'	Soft blue, with darker veins with white
'Springs Brook'	Blue-violet

Japanese irises

The flamboyant Japanese, or Ensata iris, blooms after the Bearded and Siberian irises have made their display, and what a dazzling display it offers. The enormous flat blooms atop 3- or 4-foot-high strong stems seem to float like giant butterflies over the plant. They range from single blossoms to complicated twelve-petal double blooms. Colors are white shading to blue; lavender; orchid; and rose to deep violet or purple. Patterns of white veining over dark colors are particularly beautiful. Because they are easily grown from seed, there are a great many unnamed varieties extant. Many are equally as flamboyant and captivating as the recommended varieties listed below.

VARIETY	DESCRIPTION
'Asato Birako'	Bright blue with white
'Bellender Blue'	Dark blue-violet
'Haku-Botan'	White
'Nara'	Dark purple; 9 inches across
'Oriental Fantasy'	Ruffled; white and mauve
'Pink Pearl'	Large; pale pink; darker in the middle
'Shei Shonagon'	Light blue
'Waka Murasaki'	Dark purple with white veins
'Wine Ruffles'	Large, dark red

Japanese irises do not repeat bloom.

THE WORKHORSE PERENNIAL OF THE GARDEN, SIBERIAN IRISES HAVE MANY VIRTUES—NOT THE LEAST OF WHICH IS THAT THEY COMBINE SO BEAUTIFULLY WITH OTHER SPRING FLOWERS, INCLUDING PEONIES AND AZALEAS.

Opposite: In our garden this particular Japanese iris bloomed a little late and looked lovely with Stachys (lamb's ears) and pansies. This page: The enormous, flamboyant blooms of Japanese irises.

SPURIA IRISES

Following the flamboyant Japanese, Bearded, and Siberian irises are the exotic and elegant Spurias. Resembling bulbous Dutch irises in their appearance, they offer very long lasting, stunning blooms with magical combinations of pastel and deep rich colors. They are among the taller irises, averaging 3–5 feet in height when they are happy in their location. They are used successfully as background border plants, and if content can be left without separating for decades. When left alone, they form large and very floriferous clumps, with blossoms perched atop tall stems. They are easy to grow. In recent years, they have become very popular with florists as a substitute for the Bulbous Dutch iris, and since they have a much longer vase life than the Tall Bearded iris, they are an excellent choice for arrangements. Blossoms can be kept in the refrigerator for more than a week, so they can also be used as corsages.

There are hundreds of varieties of Spuria irises, all beautiful and easily grown. Here is a list of some of the more readily available varieties.

VARIETY	DESCRIPTION
'Amber Gleam'	Amber with deeper textured veins
'Color Focus'	Violet standards, yellow falls
'Lady Butterfly'	Ruffled; lacy soft yellow
'Lavender Waves'	Ruffled; light lavender
'Royal Cadet'	Large; blue
'Snow Giant'	Large; pure white
'Sunset Colors'	Mauve-lavender with yellow
'Yellowcopter'	Deep yellow
'Zulu Chief'	Dark velvet black-red

Spuria irises do not rebloom.

RICHLY COLORED SPURIAS (ABOVE, 'ZULU CHIEF') GROW VERY TALL AND NEED STAKING. THEY WORK VERY WELL IN FLOWER ARRANGEMENTS. BELOW IS THE GLOWING 'HIGHLINE CORAL.'

LOUISIANA IRISES

Louisiana irises, native to the bayou country of Louisiana and neighboring states, were named by John James Audubon, who combined a rose-colored Louisiana iris with a Parula warbler in one of his extraordinary depictions of American birds. They are easy to grow and are available in a rainbow of colors ranging from white through many shades of lavender, blue, and violet to deepest purple. In addition, there are bitones in many shades of pink, rose, true red, bronze, and yellow, as well as bicolors and flecked and spotted varieties. They grow from 4 feet to a towering 5 feet tall. They thrive not only in the very warmest areas of the United States, but in almost every climate in the country, including the north, and grow equally happily in low-lying areas and mountains, in gardens and bogs. They are versatile when it comes to soil and garden needs. They are only now beginning to be understood and avidly sought by the general gardening community. Louisiana irises do not rebloom.

Louisiana irises, versatile, easy to grow, and colorful: 'Butterscotch Queen' (above), 'Pink Poetry' (opposite above), and 'Bayou Honey' (opposite below).

BULBOUS IRISES

Instead of growing from gnarled rhizomes, like the Bearded and Beardless irises, Bulbous irises grow from true bulbs. There are many different varieties of Bulbous irises, but we will be concerned here with only the most popular and readily available for the home gardener.

Early spring *Iris danfordiae* and *Iris reticulata* are essential for any rock garden. They bloom at the end of February and into April, depending on the region, along with *Galanthus* (snowdrops) and species crocus. Dutch and Spanish irises are also bulbous plants and bloom later in the spring. You plant the bulbs in the fall and have bloom the following spring. They are somewhat stiff in appearance, but look lovely in a spring perennial border.

IRIS DANFORDIAE AND *IRIS RETICULATA*

IRIS DANFORDIAE, a very early spring Bulbous iris, is also called Netted iris because of its net-like, paper-thin skin. These irises add a flamboyant touch of color and warmth (and a lovely violet fragrance) to the late winter garden. Among the first of all bulbs to bloom, they are perfect for rock gardens or doorway gardens where they can be viewed closely. They bloom for one or two weeks, along with *Galanthus* (snowdrops), *Eranthis* (winter aconite), tiny species crocuses, and some very early dwarf daffodils, such as 'February Gold.' They do not perennialize well, but they are so inexpensive that it is best to buy and plant new ones every fall. *Iris danfordiae* has bright sulfur-yellow blooms above 6-inch-high grasslike foliage. There is only one variety.

IRIS RETICULATA provides sparkling, late-winter color in light blue, lavender, purple, pale yellow, and white. Breeders are constantly hybridizing more and more varieties, so each year there are one or two new introductions. Here are some of the more readily available recommended varieties:

A WELCOME SIGHT ON AN EARLY SPRING DAY: VERY EARLY BLOOMING *IRIS DANFORDIAE* AND *IRIS RETICULATA* SURFACE FROM UNDER THE SNOW. SNOW DOES NOT HARM THE FLOWERS.

VARIETY	DESCRIPTION
'Cantab'	Blue with light yellow blotch on each petal
'Clairette'	Sky blue with gold markings
'Gordon'	Lobelia blue
I. reticulata	Purple-blue with violet fragrance
'Joyce'	Sky blue with a flush of orange
'J.S. Dyt'	Purplish red flowers, sweet fragrance
'Natasha'	White, sweet fragrance
'Pauline'	Deep violet-purple with a white blotch on each fall
'Pixie'	Purple

DUTCH AND SPANISH IRISES

Dutch irises are cousins to the lesser-known and less-popular Spanish irises. They are quite similar, however Dutch irises offer a more beautiful flower and are more readily available. Dutch irises grow 1–2 feet tall, and each bulb has an erect stalk, which usually has two flowers on it. Bloom time is late spring. Plant in fall along with most other bulbs. They work particularly well when planted among late-blooming tulips.

These plants, with spearlike foliage, offer some dazzling color combinations. White, yellow, orange, bronze, blue, purple, and combinations thereof are all available. Blossoms are 3–4 inches across.

Some recommended and readily available varieties are:

VARIETY	DESCRIPTION
'Carmen Beauty'	Delicate lavender with white falls and yellow blotch
'Cream Beauty'	Creamy yellow with purple margin
'Golden Beauty'	Lemon-yellow falls and orange blotch
'Gypsy Beauty'	Flax-blue standards, creamy top, yellow falls
'Oriental Beauty'	Wisteria-blue standards, bronze falls
'Rust Beauty'	Golden yellow with brownish falls
'Sapphire Beauty'	Violet standards, blue falls, yellow stripe

OTHER IRISES

There are perhaps hundreds of other varieties of irises, both in nature and commercially available. Most are quite esoteric and are rarely grown except by iris experts or hobbyists, but a few varieties are recommended for the average gardener:

IRIS PALLIDA DALMATICA 'Variegata,' a medium-height Bearded iris, is available only in purple. It has variegated foliage, which consists of green with white stripes, and is used to provide foliage contrast in iris planting. Cultivation is exactly the same as for Tall and Median Bearded iris.

IRIS BUCHARICA is a low-growing bright-yellow iris that is particularly well suited for rock gardens. It is a Bulbous iris, and after bloom, foliage dries and should be removed. Plant it in the fall, as you would I. *danfordiae* and I. *reticulata*.

THE NATIVE AMERICAN *IRIS PSEUDACORUS*, or Yellow Flag iris, blooms in May or June. An excellent bog plant, it has naturalized in the eastern part of North America and is very popular with water garden enthusiasts, though it will thrive in a dry environment as well. It is very vigorous, and must be controlled or it will take over a planting. The plants grow to 3–4 feet and in mid-spring sport profuse bright yellow blossoms, which are similar in appearance to Siberian irises. They require no special planting care. Plant anytime during the growing season, with roots and rhizomes below the surface of the soil, and all foliage above the surface.

IRIS VERSICOLOR, or Blue Flag iris, is another water-loving iris, very similar to I. *pseudacorus*, only deep blue in color. It quickly forms vigorous clumps of foliage. Flower stalks grow to around $3\frac{1}{2}$ feet over $1\frac{1}{2}$–2-foot-high foliage. They require no special planting care and will thrive in a normal environment as long as it is enriched with humus and frequently watered. As with I. *pseudacorus*, plant with roots and rhizomes beneath

47

Opposite: *Iris pallida dalmatica* 'Variegata' is grown for its foliage, but it sports a handsome flower as well. Above: A lovely display of *Iris pseudacorus* (Yellow Flag iris) with a japanese maple at Old Westbury Gardens in New York. Below: The foliage of *Iris bucharica* is almost as worthy as its flower.

the surface of the soil, with the foliage above. These are excellent for cut-flower arrangements to enjoy indoors.

IRIS TECTORUM, or Japanese Roof iris, is a member of a large class called Crested iris. The common name of these flowers derives from the fact that centuries ago in Japan, growing irises in gardens or soil was forbidden, and so people who enjoyed them grew them on their roofs. They bear lavender-blue or white flowers and grow to only 10 inches high. Both white- and blue-flowering varieties are available. Foliage grows to about 1½ feet high, with flower stalks growing about 2 feet high. Blossoms resemble those of Siberian irises. One of the few irises that thrive in shade, they are quite lovely in a spring shade garden.

OPPOSITE: THIS *IRIS PALLIDA DALMATICA* 'VARIEGATA' IS PLANTED IN FRONT OF A STRIKING *FILIPENDULA PURPUREA*. ABOVE: *IRIS TECTORUM* 'ALBA' IS BEST GROWN IN MOIST SOIL AND A SHELTERED ENVIRONMENT.

3 Growing Irises

IN MOST PARTS of the country, iris-planting time is from July through September (except for Bulbous, which are planted in the fall). Iris mail-order nurseries (see page 95) usually send their catalogues out in mid-spring. You can send in your order any time, but delivery will usually not be until the proper planting time in your area.

GETTING STARTED

BEARDED IRISES: When your order arrives, the rhizomes (with trimmed roots) will probably be packed in shredded paper or wood excelsior in a ventilated cardboard carton. Unpack the box immediately and spread the rhizomes out in a dry, shady place.

They can remain out of the ground for about a week or a little longer without serious harm, but the sooner you plant them, the better, as it is very important that their roots be well established before the growing season ends in late fall. In areas with severe winters and early freezing temperatures, plant before August 15; in warmer areas, September or October planting may be satisfactory. Check with your dealer for information about your area. Container-grown irises are often available at local garden centers and nurseries in the spring and can be planted at that time.

SIBERIAN IRISES: Siberian irises can be planted anytime during the growing season, so you probably should order your catalogues in late winter. Plants bought through a mail-order source will arrive with roots in moist wrapping of some sort. Remove the wrappings as soon as possible and soak plants in a bucket of water deep enough to cover the roots for at least twelve hours before planting. If necessary, they can stay in the water for up to a week. Change the water daily, if possible.

OUR YELLOW LABURNUM BLOOMS AT THE SAME TIME AS TALL BEARDED IRISES. SINCE THIS PICTURE WAS TAKEN WE'VE ADDED BLUE-FLOWERING CLEMATIS TO CONTRAST WITH THE YELLOW.

JAPANESE IRISES: Japanese irises are best planted in spring or fall, so start checking catalogues in late winter. It can be hard to make a selection, since they are all so beautiful. For your first experience with them, try ordering three different varieties. Once they are happily established, you will undoubtedly want more. Plants bought through a mail-order source will arrive with roots in a moist wrapping of some sort. Remove the wrapping as soon as possible and soak plants in a bucket of water deep enough to cover the roots for at least forty-eight hours to a week or more before planting. Change the water daily, if possible.

SPURIA IRISES: Order your Spuria irises from catalogues in spring or summer. Although spring planting is possible in some parts of the country, summer or fall is generally recommended. Usually, your order will arrive wrapped in a damp paper towel enclosed in a plastic bag. Plant the irises as soon as possible. If you are not quite ready to plant, either unwrap them and store them in a bucket of water for up to a week, changing the water daily, if possible—or put them—bag, paper towel, and all—in the refrigerator for up to a week, making sure the towel stays damp. Then soak them in water overnight before planting.

LOUISIANA IRISES: In most areas of the country, the best time for planting is the fall. Order any time during the year, and tell the grower that you want them shipped to you at the proper planting time for your area. Usually growers ship the rhizomes wrapped in damp paper inside a sealed plastic bag. Be sure you do not allow them to dry out before planting. If you cannot plant them right away, either unwrap them carefully and store them in a bucket full of water for as long as a week. Change the water daily, if possible. Or you can put the package as is in the refrigerator for up to a week. If you do this, soak them in water overnight before planting.

BULBOUS IRISES: When you receive your bulbs, just put them aside until the fall, when all Bulbous irises are planted. *I. danfordiae* and *I. reticulata* rarely multiply or rebloom, so they should be treated as annuals and replanted every fall. Dutch and Spanish irises do not self-propagate and are rather stiff in appearance, so they are not recommended for naturalizing but are useful in beds and borders.

SELECTING A SITE

There are two distinctly different ways to plant irises. Smaller varieties are usually worked into beds, borders, or rock gardens. Some gardeners feel that larger ones are easier to care for and make a more spectacular display if they are all planted together in an "iris garden." If you do this, you can easily use an herbicide such as Roundup (with great care so as not to spray the foliage) to keep the bed tidy. Another option is to plant tall irises as a border in a flowerbed with other perennials and annuals. They will look best at the borders or the center of the bed.

Bearded Irises: There are three factors to be considered in selecting a site for Bearded irises. First, they prefer full sun. (They will bloom in partial shade, but not as spectacularly.) Keep in mind, however, that delicately colored pink and pale-blue irises maintain their color better if planted in dappled shade, and too much sun will even prevent flowering. Second, all Bearded irises must be planted in very well-drained soil. If you do not have a well-drained spot in your garden, or if heavy rainfall is common in your area, plant on a slope or raised bed at least 6 inches high. Third, pick a spot where they will not have to compete with grass, weeds, or other plants for food and water.

Siberian Irises: Siberian irises grow best in full sun but will be successful in semi-shade, in a spot that receives a minimum of half a day of sun. It is best not to plant them where other plants or trees will compete with them for nutrients and moisture, but if you have no alternative, they should thrive reasonably well. The soil should be moist and well drained.

Japanese Irises: Japanese irises prefer a site with at least six hours of full sun a day. They do not like to be moved and will thrive for many years if they are left undisturbed. But moisture is the single most important factor in growing tall, branching plants with many large flowers. If there is insufficient water, the plants will be stunted and produce only miniature blooms. Japanese irises love boggy spots where drainage is poor; they prosper at the sides of water gardens and ponds, in areas only slightly above the water surface. If you do not have a naturally wet area, carve out a depression in the planting area; it will collect water. Alternatively, dig out the planting area to a depth of about 18 inches. Line the bottom and sides with heavy-duty rubber pond liner or another nonporous substance. Be sure that the ends of the liner extend above the soil level. Mix compost with the soil in a ratio of about two parts compost to one part soil, and water thoroughly and slowly. Once it is completely wet, plant the irises. Keep the site well watered during the growing season.

Spuria Irises: Spuria irises are grown primarily in sunny, warm climates—especially California, the Southwest, Texas, and Missouri—but can be grown successfully in almost all other U.S. climates. They require full sun and good drainage but will tolerate partial shade, especially in areas that are extremely hot in the summer. They often live for decades when they are happy in their location. If you grow other varieties of irises successfully, you should have no problem with Spurias.

Louisiana Irises: The ideal location is a spot with at least half a day of sunshine, and more if possible. In nature, Louisiana irises grow in bogs; but they also thrive in mountain areas and in beds. They can be planted in well-drained areas, in freshwater wetlands, along stream banks, and in swampy freshets that contain up to 6 inches of water.

Bulbous Irises: *Iris danfordiae* and *I. reticulata* are not fussy about light, except that they don't thrive in very deep shade. Well-drained ordinary soil is preferred. Dutch and Spanish irises should be planted in fall in ordinary soil in a spot with full sun and good drainage.

PREPARING THE SOIL

Bearded Irises: It is best to prepare the soil several weeks before planting to ensure more vigorous growth and bloom. Bearded iris roots are quite shallow, so turning over the soil to a depth of about 10 inches is sufficient. A soil pH of 6 to 7 is recommended, but since irises are quite adaptable to different pHs, it is usually not necessary to amend the soil.

Since irises prefer light and friable soil, if your soil is like clay, dig in a considerable amount of coarse sand, as well as compost, humus, or gypsum. A ratio of about two parts soil to one part additive is sufficient to improve drainage. A low-nitrogen fertilizer such as 5-5-10 (at the rate of 1 pound per 50 square feet) should also be added. Never use a high-nitrogen fertilizer, and use manure only if it has been aged for about a year and is worked 6–8 inches deep in the bed.

Extra food is necessary for the very best growth and bloom of your irises. For a new planting, a low-nitrogen chemical fertilizer or super phosphate can be dug into the soil at the rate of ½ ounce per square foot three weeks before the plants are set in. Half this amount should be used if it is added just before planting time.

SIBERIAN IRISES: Siberian irises prefer a rich soil with ample organic matter. If the soil is clayey, add organic matter to help loosen it. If the soil is sandy, the organic matter will help retain water and nutrients. Till in manure, hay, straw, peat moss, compost, or wood chips at a rate of one part additive to five parts soil. If using hay, straw, or wood chips, you may need to add high-nitrogen fertilizer. Adding some peat humus (Michigan peat) works well in a small garden. The soil should be slightly acid (pH 5.5 to 6.5), but don't be too concerned about the soil, as Siberian irises are not fussy and will grow vigorously even under conditions that are far less than optimal.

JAPANESE IRISES: Fortify the planting area with a lot of humus-rich soil and sphagnum peat moss. This will not only help acidify the soil— these irises prefer a slightly acidic pH—but it will also help retain the moisture that is so crucial to the plant's performance. Also add compost and well-rotted manure. Do not add granular fertilizers until plants are well established.

SPURIA IRISES: Soil pH should be neutral to slightly alkaline, so add lime to acid soils. For superior plants and flower stalks, incorporate plenty of well-rotted manure and/or commercial fertilizer into the soil since Spurias are very heavy feeders.

LOUISIANA IRISES: To grow Louisiana irises, it is best to have an acid bed with a great deal of moisture. A soil pH of 6.5—the same that azaleas, camellias, and rhododendrons favor—is ideal. Dig the soil and add large amounts of well-rotted compost, sphagnum peat moss, and other organic matter. Plan on using a full wheelbarrow of additive over 6–8 square feet of garden area.

BULBOUS IRISES: No soil preparation is necessary for I. *danfordiae* and I. *reticulata*, as all the food they need for their one- or two-season blooming period is stored in the bulb. For Dutch and Spanish irises, add well-rotted compost, sphagnum peat moss, or other organic matter at the rate of one part additive to three parts soil and work it in 1 foot deep.

PLANTING

BEARDED IRISES: Before you begin, be sure you know exactly which varieties you are going to plant. Have a list of what you have ordered, with colors, height, and patterns all noted. If the bed is to be viewed as a border from one side only, plant the taller varieties in the back. If the bed is to be an "island," plant the taller varieties in the middle. Do not plant irises that are similar in color right next to each other, because the impact of both is considerably diminished by proximity.

The most important thing to consider when planting Bearded irises is to be sure that the planting is not too deep. The soil should always just cover the top of the rhizome. In fact, it is best to have some of the top surface just visible above the soil level. The depth of the planting hole depends upon the size and variety of the rhizome. For Tall Bearded irises, when you plant, make a 3-inch deep depression about 6 inches in diameter in the soil. In the center make a small mound. Place the rhizome on top of the mound, so that about a third of it is above the soil level. Spread the roots out into the depressed areas, and replace the soil, being sure that it is firmly packed. Then give the new planting plenty of water.

Naturally, Miniature and Dwarf varieties will require a shallower hole. You can judge this by looking carefully at the rhizome and determining how large or small it is. Dig a hole deep enough so that the top of the rhizome will be slightly above the soil surface. For a mass of color and an instant clump, plant at least three rhizomes in a triangle with each fan of leaves pointed away from the center. Miniature and Dwarf varieties can be set closer together (2–4 inches apart) than Tall Bearded varieties (8–10 inches apart).

If you are planting a large iris bed, dig two shallow trenches with a mound or ridge between them. Set the rhizome on the mound, spread the roots out in the trenches, and pack the soil tightly. Then fill the depressions around the mound with soil, being sure that the top of the rhizome is just barely beneath or even showing above the soil. (In very hot areas, it is best to cover the iris rhizome with about an inch of soil.) If you are planting several rhizomes, space them about 2–4 inches apart for Miniature and Dwarf varieties and 8–10 inches apart for larger varieties. New growth will fill in between the plants in about three years.

New plantings need water to help root systems get established. If your climate is dry, occasional deep watering is better than more frequent shallow watering. Established irises normally do not need to be watered, except in very dry areas. Overwatering promotes rot diseases.

It is a good idea for the first winter to provide only newly planted rhizomes with some protection to prevent heaving. Mulch lightly, but do not cover the rhizome. Avoid using grass clippings or other mulches that may pack down and trap moisture around the plant. In colder areas, it is a good idea to provide some physical protection against heaving, particularly with the Miniature and Standard Dwarfs and the medium-sized varieties. A good way to do this is to place a brick or stone over the rhizome after the first frost; pin larger ones in place with a U-shaped holder made from a wire clothes hanger. You can mulch Median irises with salt hay or straw (or even builder's sand) but once winter is over, be sure to remove all mulch, which may cause rot.

Bearded irises prefer a summer or early fall planting.

SIBERIAN IRISES: Plant at any time during the growing season at a time when you and the weather will be able to keep the soil wet continuously until new growth appears. The tops of the rhizomes should be 1–2 inches below the surface of the soil. Plant on a ridge or mound, with the roots spread down the mound. Fill in the soil and firm it down, leaving no air pockets under the rhizome. Encircle each plant with a well 1–3 inches deep to help retain water. Water thoroughly and do not allow newly planted Siberians to become dry until completely established.

JAPANESE IRISES: Japanese irises should be planted in spring or fall. Once you have prepared your soil, plant the rhizomes 2–3 inches deep in a depression. If the soil is light, plant 3 inches deep; if heavy, plant 2 inches deep. Keep the planting well watered during the rest of the growing season.

SPURIA IRISES: Dig a 6–8-inch-deep hole and fill with good-quality compost. Plant the rhizome 1 inch below the soil level in heavy soil and 2 inches deep in light, sandy soil. Space plants 2 feet apart to give them room to grow into large clumps. You can expect top performance by the third year after planting. Plant in the fall.

Louisiana Irises: Plant anytime from late summer through early fall so that the plant will be established before winter weather sets in. Set the rhizomes 1 inch below the surface of the soil, space them 12–18 inches apart, and water heavily to remove any air pockets around the planting. Mulch heavily, preferably with pine needles.

To grow Louisiana irises in water, place three rhizomes of one variety in an 18-inch diameter pot that is at least 8 inches deep. Plant the rhizomes 2 inches beneath the soil surface. Place the pot in water, with its surface no more than 6 inches below the surface of the water.

Bulbous Irises: Bulbous irises are very easy to plant. For *I. reticulata* and *I. danfordiae*, loosen the soil down to 6 inches deep and plant the bulbs in holes 2–3 inches deep, 3–4 inches apart. Dutch and Spanish irises, which work particularly well in the garden among late-blooming tulips, should be planted 3–4 inches deep and 3–4 inches apart.

FERTILIZING

Bearded Irises: For the most spectacular bloom and disease prevention, it is important to fertilize your iris bed. But do so in moderation! The three basic elements in fertilizer—nitrogen, potassium, and phosphorus—are essential for vigorous growth, but too much nitrogen encourages foliage growth, which makes the plant more susceptible to pests and diseases. At planting time and then every year, early in spring and again in early summer following bloom, fertilize with 5-10-10 or 6-10-6 fertilizer or super phosphate, but never use a fertilizer heavy in nitrogen. Just sprinkle a handful—about 1/3 to 1/2 cup of fertilizer—in a circle around each clump. Do this just before a rain, which will wash away any fertilizer that may have fallen on new growth, or just hose the plants clean. Rebloomers should be fertilized in the same way.

60

Siberian Irises: At planting time, fertilize very lightly (one teaspoon of 5-10-5 per plant), or not at all. The later you plant in the fall, the less fertilizer you should use, if any. Never use high-nitrogen fertilizers, which encourage leaf growth and discourage blooming, or fresh manure,

which will burn the roots and crown of the plant. Siberian irises are moderate feeders. Once the plants are established, a liberal application of a balanced fertilizer, such as 10-10-10, in spring and just after bloom is beneficial. Many of the pros add some alfalfa pellets or alfalfa meal to the soil. Besides its low concentration of nutrients, alfalfa contains triacontanol, which is a natural growth stimulant.

Japanese Irises: Once established, Japanese irises generally thrive. But they are heavy feeders, so at planting time and every spring thereafter scratch in a good handful of 5-10-5 fertilizer around each plant.

Spuria Irises: If fertilized properly, clumps will persist and bloom for years—ten or fifteen years is not unusual—and eventually spread to as much as 5–6 feet. Use a balanced fertilizer that is high in phosphate

Tall Bearded irises bloom in front of our 1812 carriage house. They will soon be joined by peonies.

(16-16-16 or 16-20-0) to encourage heavy bloom. Apply at planting time, in the spring after bloom, and every fall thereafter. Also apply a solution of Miracle-Gro several times in the fall and early spring. If your soil is heavy, apply a generous layer of compost or mulch around the plants.

Louisiana Irises: Several good feedings of commercial fertilizer should be applied in early fall, when the roots are developing, and in very early spring, about two months before blooming. Use 8-8-8, 6-12-6, or 5-10-5 fertilizer, and scratch it into the soil at the rate of about 2–3 pounds per 100 square feet. Avoid placing fertilizer directly on top of the rhizomes. And it is also a good idea, starting in early spring and continuing on through the bloom season, to feed the bed with an acid food such as Miracid, at the strength recommended on the package.

Bulbous Irises: Fertilizer is not necessary for *Iris danfordiae* and *I. reticulata*, as the fertilizer is in the bulb. For Dutch and Spanish irises, when shoots emerge in the second spring and every spring thereafter, scratch in one tablespoon of 9-9-6 fertilizer per square foot of planting area.

CARE AND MAINTENANCE

Bearded Irises: In the spring, when Tall Bearded and some Intermediate irises sport stalks, it is a good idea to stake each one with a bamboo stake. The stalks of these two varieties usually are not strong enough to support their heavy blossoms and thus may break or bend to the ground in a heavy rain. Get both 36-inch and 24-inch sticks, and as a blossom stalk begins to emerge, sink a stake into the ground next to it. Then when the stalk is halfway grown, attach it to the stake with paper-covered wire strips. When the stalk is full grown, use two or three per stake.

After the clumps are finished blooming, remove the spent flower stalks. Cut them with a sharp knife to an inch or two above the rhizome. This prevents seed formation and channels the energy into growth for next year's bloom. Any dead, browned, or diseased leaves on the plants should also be cut off, preferably with shears, for they make a clean cut. Be sure to dispose of all gathered debris; do not compost it.

If the spring is very dry, water the plants often enough to keep the soil moist but not wet. Bearded irises thrive with only 1 inch of water a week. It is not a good idea to water from overhead, as this wets the foliage and encourages pests and diseases, and it is far better to give them too little than too much water. In early spring and again in the fall, clean up dead leaves and other debris that may have accumulated around the plants. This helps to minimize pests and diseases. And the iris bed will look better if it is tidy.

Do not use any mulch to control weeds during the growing season, as iris rhizomes may rot. You can cultivate around the plants, but only to a depth of 1–2 inches, without disturbing the roots of the plant. Do not use general grass-weed killers, as many will also damage irises. If you want to spray with glysophate (Roundup), protect the irises from the spray with a piece of cardboard. Spray only on a day when there is no wind, set the spray to the minimum level, and wash any errant spray from the foliage. To be totally safe, hand weed the bed.

Rebloomers must be watered regularly in order to rebloom. Before flowering, water plants often enough to keep the soil moist but not wet.

SIBERIAN IRISES: During the growing season, cultivate regularly to control weeds and clear away garden debris. Use straw, rotted sawdust, pine needles, or wood chips—not peat moss or grass clippings—as mulch, 1–3 inches deep, to retain moisture, keep weeds down, and generally dress up the flowerbed. Once established and mulched, most Siberians can get along with as little water as Bearded irises and can withstand drought with minimal supplemental water. More water, however, is also all right.

After bloom, cut off the stalks near the ground on a dry, sunny day. Or leave them and their attractive seedpods in place either till fall or right through the winter. Siberian irises are tough and need no winter protection, except for newly planted divisions in very cold climates. They are moderate feeders. A liberal application of a balanced fertilizer, such as 10-10-10, in spring and just after bloom is beneficial.

JAPANESE IRISES: Keep plants weed free during the growing season and remove all spent blossoms. Mulch with organic material or wood chips to a depth of 2–3 inches and leave the mulch there all year round. They need extra water in the spring, before bloom, but be sure that plants are regularly watered all summer long. Never let the soil dry out. Remove stalks when blooms are spent.

SPURIA IRISES: To keep the bed looking tidy after bloom, you can cut back spent stalks as well as old leaves. Do not water in July and August, as Spurias like to go through a dormant period, and too much moisture combined with summer heat can cause a rot that destroys new growth. The first fall after planting, mulch plants with a layer of compost or well-rotted manure to feed them and protect them from the cold of the first winter. In the late fall, cut the foliage down to about 1 inch and clean all around the clump to get ready for next spring's growth.

LOUISIANA IRISES: Mulch heavily all year round to preserve moisture and to protect the plants from sun scald, which can bring on deterioration and rot. Place 2–4 inches of pine needles, pine straw, semi-rotted leaves, or cypress shavings on the bed. (If you plant your Louisiana irises in water, you need not be concerned with mulching or sun scald.) Once the plant has bloomed, continue to mulch as above and water heavily. A lot of moisture is essential to success with this variety. The two most crucial times during the growing season for water are in the fall and the

PINK ASTILBE AND FLOWING JAPANESE IRISES MOVE GRACEFULLY WITH THE WIND.

early spring, about two months prior to blooming. Don't forget that one thorough soaking a week is better for all plants than more frequent light sprinklings.

Try to keep the bed free of grass and weeds. Cultivate shallowly, as the roots of the plant are very near the surface of the soil. After bloom, cut stalks off 1 inch above the base of the plant.

Bulbous Irises: *Iris danfordiae* and *Iris reticulata*: Water only if spring season is dry. After bloom, the plant is dormant. Dutch and Spanish irises: Water heavily from the time when leaves emerge from soil in early spring until about one month after flowers fade. Then do not water, and allow foliage to dry.

PESTS AND DISEASE

Although most irises are tough and rarely succumb to disease, you will have to look out for minor infestations.

Bearded Irises: Bearded irises are usually quite free of pests and diseases, but some can occasionally be tricky, particularly in humid climates. By using a combination of cultural, organic, and pesticide controls, the following pests and diseases can be controlled reasonably well.

Leaf spot: After Bearded irises have bloomed, leaves may become dotted with small, brown spots with a watery, streaked appearance. Margins around the spots turn yellow. This fungus will not do significant harm to plants if it occurs in small amounts, but if it gets out of hand, it can weaken the leaves and thus the plant.

To avoid fungal leaf spot, plant irises in full sun in a rich, well-drained soil, and always keep your garden tidy. Be sure there is sufficient air circulation around the plants. Remove all withered foliage and get rid of weeds. Avoid wetting the foliage when watering. Do not work among plants when the foliage is wet.

If fungus strikes, remove all dead and diseased leaves, and spray with a registered systemic fungicide during extended periods of high humidity or rain. Do this every seven to ten days to protect young growth. A spreader sticker or surfactant can be used to make the fungicide adhere to the foliage and ensure good coverage.

Some members of the American Iris Society have suggested a non-

65

chemical spray. This spray does prevent mildew and may work on leaf spot as well. To a gallon of water, add 3 tablespoons baking soda, 2 tablespoons of shavings from a bar of Ivory soap, and 1 tablespoon vegetable oil. Apply the spray to infected parts of plants.

Iris Borers: The most threatening of the Bearded iris pests are iris borers. They are most prevalent in the northeast and adjoining areas, but are not confined to that part of the country. The eggs are laid in the fall on leaves and overwinter there. They hatch in late April, and the tiny caterpillars crawl up iris leaves and begin chewing their way down within the leaf fold. The first sure signs of their presence are small, ragged notches on the leaf edge or small accumulations of sawdust-like frass (borer excrement) in early spring. The borers make their way into the leaf fans and eat down to the rhizomes. They often consume the entire rhizome, leaving only a shell. The leaves turn yellow and pull out easily. In the summer, the mature borer caterpillars leave the rhizomes and lay eggs in the surrounding earth. About a month later, grayish-brown moths hatch and lay their eggs on dead leaves and garden debris. The eggs overwinter, and the whole process repeats.

As with leaf spot above, the best way to avoid this problem is to remove all withered foliage and debris next to and near the iris planting. Do this both in spring and in late fall, as this is where the evil eggs overwinter. Do not compost the debris, but dispose of it in the garbage. In the spring, when new growth starts, you can spray the leaves with an insecticide. Both dimethoate (Cygon 2E), which is a powerful systemic insecticide, and lindane are used for this purpose. Spray when new growth is 6–9" high. If borers persist (or just to be on the safe side), spray a second time ten days later. You can do this up until bloom time. Also, feel the leaves. If you sense a lump that might be a borer, squeeze it and kill the worm. If the problem is advanced, dig the rhizomes after bloom, usually in July or August, and physically remove the borers or squeeze them to death in your gloved fingers.

Bacterial Soft Rot: Although not nearly as common as leaf spot or iris borer infestation, bacterial soft rot can be a very serious problem unless

A MONUMENTAL BEARDED IRIS SOARING INTO THE BLUE SKY.

treated. Here is what happens: Bacteria enter the rhizome through surface injuries or cuts, such as those that iris borers inflict on the rhizome. A yellow ooze and soft rot then sets in and causes the rhizomes to become disgustingly mushy and smelly. If the problem is just beginning, remove the mushy leaves. If it's extensive, dig up the rhizome and remove all of the mushy tissue. Then, with a sharp clean knife, cut off the diseased parts. Wipe the knife after each cut and disinfect it in a 10–12 percent solution of household bleach. After surgery, soak the rhizome in the bleach solution for several minutes, rinse it off, and place it in the sun and open air until it is dry. Then replant. If the rot is very extensive, dig up the rhizomes and throw them in the garbage.

As with the above problems, prevention is the best cure. Here are some tips. Always plant Bearded iris rhizomes so that their top surface is at or just beneath soil level. You should be able to see some of the rhizome after planting. Be sure you have selected a site with good drainage. Do not mulch or fertilize heavily, and avoid using fresh manure or fertilizers, which are heavy in nitrogen content. Control borers.

Crown Rot or Mustard-Seed Fungus: Crown rot fungus strikes rarely, but if it does you will notice rot at the base of the leaves just above the rhizome. Leaves fall over. Rust-colored matter resembling mustard seeds is produced by the fungus, evident on the surface of the rhizome and leaf bases. To control, trim all leaves to about 6–8 inches to allow more sunlight and air circulation. Remove and destroy all leaves that show evidence of the disease.

SIBERIAN IRISES: Mercifully, there are no major diseases or insects that attack Siberian irises.

JAPANESE IRISES: Although borers, thrips, and other pests are rarely a problem with Japanese irises, it is a good idea to keep your iris bed tidy and weed free. And in the fall, remove all foliage to help control insects and diseases.

SPURIA IRISES: Pests and diseases strike rarely, but ants sometimes like Spurias' sweet nectar. You may want to use ant stakes at the base of the plant, if it becomes a problem.

Viruses affect some Spuria irises, although almost never fatally. They can cause some disfigurement of the plant, petals, and texture.

There is no known cure, so when making your selection, look for virus-resistant varieties.

Very rarely, mustard-seed fungus strikes. Once it gets started in a clump the whole clump is doomed. If this fungus is present in your area, the best solution is to sprinkle powdered fungicide called Terraclor on the soil before planting. Check with your local cooperative extension about this.

Louisiana Irises: Louisiana irises have few pests or enemies, but rust can strike early-blooming varieties. It is usually best to discard infected plants, in the garbage, not the compost heap. Also, cover rhizomes with mulch to avoid sun scald.

Bulbous Irises: *Iris danfordiae* and *Iris reticulata* are rodent proof. Dutch and Spanish irises are not rodent proof, but there are no insects or diseases that attack these varieties.

DIVIDING AND TRANSPLANTING

Bearded Irises: Sometime after its third year, Bearded iris bloom will diminish substantially. This means it's time to divide the irises—to remove the new side shoots that grew off the original rhizome.

You do this one to two months after bloom, in July and August in most parts of the country. It is easiest to dig the entire structure out of the ground with a spading fork, and then clean the soil from the root system. Cut the new rhizomes from the old—it no longer produces leaves and flowers—and discard the old rhizome and foliage in the garbage. Do not compost them. Use a very sharp knife and dip it into a 10 percent bleach solution to kill any bacteria after every cut.

Cut back the foliage to about 6 inches high, which will help the plants retain moisture, and inspect them for signs of damage due to iris borer or soft rot. If they have borers but are not damaged badly, physically remove the borers. If they are mildly infected with soft rot, scrape out the affected tissue, dip the rhizomes in a solution that is one part bleach and nine parts water, rinse, and allow them to dry before replanting. Many experienced iris growers also dust the wounds with a scouring powder such as Comet. The chlorine in Comet kills any bacteria. Others soak the new rhizomes in a solution of one part chlorine to ten parts water. Many growers suggest letting the new rhizomes sit in the sun for a a period of 4–6 hours before you replant them.

Each division should consist of a vigorous, firm rhizome and a fan of healthy leaves. Either replant all of the new plants or share them with family and friends, almost always a welcome gift.

If you are replanting the irises in the same location, take out some of the old soil and check it for borers and borer pupae, removing and destroying as necessary. Add new soil mixed with compost or aged manure.

Replant them about 8–18 inches apart. (Dwarf and Miniature Irises can be planted closer together.) Plant divisions of the same variety in a triangle with the fans facing outward. This helps to give a good display the first blooming season. Tamp the soil around the roots very firmly to keep newly planted iris from being damaged by wind and being pulled from the soil. Keep plants well watered during hot spells. If you live in an area where winter freezing and thawing results in heaving plants out of the ground, cover your entire planting with salt hay. Be sure to remove it early in the spring when new growth commences.

DIVIDING IRISES

1

2

3

4

70

1. MIX 5-10-10 OR 6-10-6 FERTILIZER INTO THE SOIL.
2. CUT AN OVERGROWN CLUMP OF IRISES INTO MANAGEABLE SECTIONS. CUT THE LEAVES BACK TO ABOUT 6 INCHES IN LENGTH.

3. CUT BACK ⅔ OF THE LENGTH OF THE ROOTS.
4. PLANT IN A CIRCLE OF FIVE FOR A BIG DISPLAY OR A TRIANGLE OF THREE, BARELY COVERING THE RHIZOMES.

In general, if you treat the irises as you would newly planted rhizomes, the plants will do just fine, and new blossom stalks will emerge after a year or so.

If you have to move your irises, do so only from July to September.

Siberian Irises: Vigorous Siberians should be divided every three years, or they will bloom sparsely. In addition, they become more difficult to divide as they grow larger. Divide them using the two-pitchfork method, inserting the forks in the middle of the plant and slowly easing them apart. According to Rita Gormley of Gormley Greenery, Siberians are notoriously slow to recover from transplanting, so the less shock to the plant, the more quickly it will begin blooming again. Leave as much dirt as you can on the divisions, never let them dry out, and get them back into the ground as soon as possible. Each division should have three to six foliage fans once divided and replanted. Mulch them, feed them with Miracid, and water regularly.

More moderately growing varieties can remain undivided for five years or more. Plant these irises in a naturally moist area, or in an area where you can water the new plants until they become established. Planting in a small depression (1 to 3 inches below the average soil level) will help the plant receive extra water during rains or when watered. The roots should not be allowed to dry out during transplanting. Do the planting in the cool of the evening if possible. If the weather is very hot, it might help to shade new transplants in some way.

Japanese Irises: Each year new roots grow above the previous year's roots. In three or four years, when the roots can be seen, dig and divide the plant. Replant in a new area, or amend the soil by fortifying it with compost or rotted manure, at a ratio of about four parts soil to one part additive. Once the plants are established, feed Miracid or Hollytone, according to directions on the package. Do this only in early spring, and don't forget that during the first season, newly planted divided irises need heavy watering to thrive.

Transplant Japanese irises anytime from spring until fall, so long as you keep the transplants wet for the rest of the year. When dividing, cut back three-quarters of the plant's foliage and divide into two to four fan divisions. Do not let divisions dry out. Soak in a bucket of water for up to forty-eight hours before planting.

Spuria Irises: If you decide to move Spuria irises be sure to keep the roots and rhizomes moist after digging. This is very important; if plants dry out, they will die. Wrap them in a wet towel or newspaper and place them in a plastic bag and put it in the refrigerator. You can leave them there for as long as three or four months. In fact, such long refrigeration will enhance an early bloom the first year. Space them far enough apart so that they grow in the same location for years, as Spuria irises resent being transplanted and usually do not bloom the first year after planting. The second year you will be rewarded with several blossom stalks. Spuria irises grow steadily and noninvasively, so it is rarely necessary to divide them.

Louisiana Irises: To keep Louisiana irises vigorous, dig up the entire clump every three or four years in August. Divide by either breaking off new rhizomes or cutting them off with a sharp knife. Be sure that each cutting has at least one fan with foliage or a swollen bud. Trim foliage into an inverted V shape, and discard old rhizomes. Replant as above.

Transplant Louisiana irises in late summer.

Bulbous Irises: It is not necessary to divide Bulbous irises.

OTHER IRISES

Iris pallida dalmatica 'Variegata'
Cultivation is exactly the same as for Tall and Median Bearded irises.

Iris bucharica
After bloom, foliage dries and should be removed. Plant this bulbous plant in the fall, as you would *Iris danfordiae* and *Iris reticulata*. (See Bulbous Irises.)

Iris pseudacorus (Yellow Flag iris)
These require no special planting care and will thrive not only in a bog but in a normal dry environment as well. Plant anytime during the growing season, with all roots and rhizomes below the surface of the soil, and all foliage above the surface of soil.

Iris versicolor (Blue Flag iris)

No special planting care is required. These will thrive in a normal environment as long as it is enriched with humus and frequently watered. As with *I. pseudacorus*, plant with roots and rhizomes beneath the surface of the soil, and foliage above.

Iris tectorum (Japanese Roof Iris)

These thrive in shade—one of the few irises that do—and are quite lovely in a spring shade garden.

Spuria iris 'Strike One' has long-lasting, stunning blooms and is easy to grow. If fertilized properly, Spuria irises will bloom for years.

4 Irises in the Landscape

WITH ALL THE varieties of irises that are available, no one should be without them in the garden. Dwarf *I. reticulata* and I. *danfordiae* are ideal for rock gardens, dressing up early spring dooryards. Intermediate Bearded irises are excellent for cutting and very practical since you do not have to stake individual stalks. Tall Bearded are dramatic and flamboyant, and although a little more work than others, well worth it. Siberians, Japanese, and Louisianas bloom in late spring and early summer and work well in wetland environments as well as normal soils.

You can install an iris planting virtually anywhere you want in your landscape. They work particularly well:

In flower beds
In flower or shrub borders
Along driveways
Along walks
In rock gardens
At the front of walls
In front of evergreen hedges
Along fences
Around birdbaths, sundials, or other garden ornaments

Of course, if you are going to invest time and money in an iris planting, you will want it to be in harmony with your landscape and to add beauty to your home and surroundings. Although rules are made to be broken, here are a few basics to help you landscape with irises.

Always plant at least three of the Medium and Tall Bearded irises together, preferably all the same color. Low-growing Dwarf irises should also be planted in groups of no fewer than three.

Never buy a rainbow mixture of irises. The result at bloom time will be a hodgepodge of color, ineffective and often messy looking.

THE PASTEL COLORS OF IRISES AND LUPINES COMBINE TO CREATE A SOOTHING EFFECT.

Avoid planting in a straight line or in a single circle around a tree or bush, for the result will look ridiculous and unnatural.

Siberian Irises are excellent landscape plants, easy to grow, appreciating mulch, with elegant vertical blue-green foliage that looks good throughout the growing season.

Other irises work well in specimen plantings or in borders, although in many cases mulch should be avoided. The large and impressive flowers of the Tall Bearded have made it a garden favorite. However, some shorter varieties are excellent choices in areas where wind may topple the taller ones. Miniature Tall Bearded clumps often send up many stalks to create a beautiful garden plant, looking good even after a few stalks are cut for the table.

Louisianas, Japanese, and I. pseudacorus will flourish in wet environments, even in shallow water. Siberians grow well nearby, but do best where there is no standing water.

When planning an iris scheme, concentrate on two or three colors in each location, but do not mix them together. For example, a cluster or drift of purple irises next to a drift of yellow and a drift of white irises looks more harmonious than one cluster each of violet, orange, red, pink, yellow, and white.

Decide if you want a formal- or informal-looking iris garden and then stick to your decision. Keep in mind that an informal garden is asymmetrical and is thus more appropriate for the majority of residences. Few of us live in houses so stately that a formal planting is called for.

Remember that Dutch irises are stately, formal, and somewhat rigid in appearance, so use them sparingly unless you want a very formal look.

Consider the landscape not only from the outdoors point of view, but also from indoors, through windows. Since early Bulbous and Miniature and Standard Bearded irises begin blooming from late February through March or early April in most parts of the country and continue through the spring, plant so that you can enjoy them from inside as well as outside.

PLANNING YOUR IRIS PLANTING

You can plan your design on graph paper; this method is excellent for tulips and other bulbs. But I have found that it is easier and more effective to lay out the irises themselves where I want to plant them, and then I make a rough diagram of the planting for future reference. Usually, when you order irises from mail-order sources, the names of the varieties are written with indelible black pen on foliage, or a wooden tie-on is attached. I find that both disappear after the first year. So I buy cheap plastic forks, write the names on the forks in indelible pen, and then stick them in the ground after planting the irises. They last for years.

There are two approaches to planning your iris garden. First you can plant lots of different kinds of irises that extend the bloom season—starting with I. danfordiae and I. reticulata, then the Dwarf Standards and Miniature, Beardeds, Siberians, and Japanese—and then starting over again with rebloomers. To enhance your plantings select carefree, noninvasive perennials that bloom earlier or later than the irises to fill in with color both before and after the iris display. Or you can stick to one variety of iris—for example, Tall Bearded—and once the display is over, plant annuals between them.

In either case, be sure to use caution in companion plantings. Bearded irises need free air circulation around their foliage and resent crowding and competition. Companion plants should be widely spaced, as should the iris clumps, to avoid leaf spot and rhizome rot.

If you plan to intersperse perennials or early-blooming annuals such as pansies in a border of early irises, consider their foliage colors. Remember that a plant without flowers during the spring tulip season can provide green, silvery, gray, or even blue foliage and thus provide color even when not in bloom.

Always think about the color, texture, and shape of the foliage when you select perennials or annuals to plant with your iris. If a certain variety sports a beautiful flower, but its foliage is problematical or ugly, avoid it. Remember that most plants bear flowers for only a short period during the growing season while foliage, with a few exceptions, is present throughout the season. Some varieties of perennials are evergreen and add interest to your border or bed during the winter and early spring months, when the first iris blooms.

COLOR IN YOUR GARDEN

Much has been written about planning a garden that is harmonious in color. I'll include some very basic information here, to help you get started. The color wheel consists of the three primary colors—red, blue, and yellow—and the three secondary colors—purple, green, and orange. Use the color wheel to help plan the color scheme of your garden. Keep in mind that when a color is specified, that means all shades of that color; "red," for example, means pink, carmine, scarlet, etc. And remember that at least one-fourth of the planting should be white.

If purple is your main color, concentrate on using the adjacent colors on the wheel—that is, blue and red of all shades—along with white. An occasional accent can be provided by the opposite color on the wheel—in this case, yellow. If you select yellow as your main color, concentrate on using the adjacent orange and green along with white when you select blossom color; in this case, purple can provide the occasional accent. And so on. Always keep in mind that all rules are made to be broken.

EFFECTIVE COLOR COMBINATIONS

Different colors of irises combine very well with each other, but there are some classic combinations that you might want to consider. Various shades of purple, blue, and pink work especially well with all varieties of Bearded irises. But be sure to allow for pure white irises to break up the colors. If space is limited, you might try making an in-ground bouquet, mixing irises of compatible colors.

'Chico Maid' (pale blue), 'Olympiad' (pale violet blue), 'Breakers' (deep blue), 'Mulled Wine' (rich burgundy), and 'Star Crest' (pale violet) work particularly well together.

Bicolors are also effective, especially if white is the second color: 'Blue Staccato' (blue and white), 'Rare Treat' (white edged in blue), 'Sierra Grande' (white standards with blue falls), 'Jazzed Up' (white standards with violet falls), 'Mary Frances' (medium violet), and

'Feature Attraction' (medium violet with white).

A yellow-and-gold mix can also be very effective. Try 'Elegant Impression' (pale yellow standards with white falls), 'Overjoyed' (lemon yellow with white), 'Spiced Custard' (yellow standards with orange falls), 'Throb' (gold with orange beards), and 'Millennium Sunrise' (yellow-orange with orange beards).

While you browse through catalogues to select the color combinations for your garden, remember that there are scores of different irises to choose from at many different price ranges. Higher cost most definitely does not mean higher quality. (Most often it is an indicator that the iris is new, recently hybridized, and scarce.)

If you select from blue, purple, pink, and white, you can rarely go wrong. The mahogany, gold, orange, and brown ranges work well together, but do not mix well with blue, purple, and pink.

With Beardless irises, you can rarely go wrong. The color ranges available in Siberians, Spuria, Louisiana, and Japanese irises all work well together. The same can be said for Bulbous irises.

COMPANION PLANTINGS FOR EARLY-BLOOMING IRISES

Some early bulbs that are good companions for Miniature and Standard Dwarf Bearded and *Iris danfordiae* and *I. reticulata* are:

PLANT	DESCRIPTION
Anemone 'de Caen'	Red, white, pink, blue, purple
Bulbocodium vernum	Pale lavender
Crocus, Dutch	Gold, blue, white, purple, silver
Crocus, Species	White, cream, yellow, purple, blue, lilac
Daffodil, Miniature	'February Gold' is the earliest; yellow, white, gold
Eranthis (Winter aconite)	Buttercup-shaped; yellow
Galanthus (Snowdrop)	White
Muscari (Grape hyacinth)	White or deep blue
Tulip, Greigii, Kaufmanniana, or species	Many colors

ABOVE: IN MAY EARLY-BLOOMING STANDARD DWARF IRISES AND *PULMONARIA* 'MRS. MOON' ENHANCE THE LOOK OF OUR WATER GARDEN. OTHER IRISES IN THE BACKGROUND WILL PROVIDE MORE COLOR DURING THE WEEKS TO COME. BELOW: A STATUE OF ST. FRANCIS LOOKS DOWN AT BLOOMING MINIATURE DWARF BEARDED IRISES, CANDYTUFT, CREEPING THYME, PHLOX, AND HENS AND CHICKS.

EARLY-BLOOMING PERENNIALS AS IRIS COMPANIONS

Since it is too early for annuals when the earliest iris blooms, here is a list of early-blooming perennials that are appropriate as iris companions. These all work especially well in a rock garden or low-growing border area.

PLANT	DESCRIPTION
Aethionema x warleyense (Warley Rose)	Pink
Ajuga	Deep blue
Alyssum 'Citrum'	Pale yellow
Alyssum saxatile	Brilliant sulfur yellow
Alyssum 'Sunny Border Apricot'	Apricot
Anemone pulsatilla	White, red, or purple; bell-shaped
Arabis	Mounds of clusters of white
Armeria (Thrift)	Deep rose; pincushion-shaped
Asperula (Sweet woodruff)	Small; white
Aubrieta (Rock cress)	Mounds of purple, blue, or white
Brunnera macrophylla (Forget-me-not)	Blue
Dicentra eximia	Pink; pantaloon-shaped
Doronicum	Bright yellow; daisy-shaped
Draba sibirica	Tiny; yellow
Echiveria (Hens and chicks)	Succulent; pink, green, jade, red foliage
Helleborus orientalis (Lenten rose)	Pink
Iberis (Candytuft)	Clusters of white
Lamium maculatum	Clusters of white
Mertensia virginica	Blue, bell-shaped
Primula	Yellow, rust, red, pink, blue, purple
Pulmonaria angustifolia	Yellow
Pulmonaria 'Mrs. Moon'	Small blue blossoms
Sedum	Yellow, pink, white small
Stachys byzantina (Lamb's ears)	Silver foliage
Trillium grandiflorum	Large white blossoms
Viola	Blue, apricot, yellow, purple, white

COMPLEMENTING MID-SEASON AND LATE-BLOOMING IRIS PLANTINGS

As the season progresses, more and more early-blooming perennials flower. These can be used to great advantage in planning an iris garden. All perennials can be planted in spring or fall.

PLANT	DESCRIPTION
Allium	Many different colors and heights
Anemone blanda	White, blue, pink, purple; daisy-like blooms
Camassia	Feathery blue spikes
Chionodoxa (Glory-of-the-snow)	Blue with white eye
Convallaria (Lily-of-the-valley)	White; bell-shaped
Daffodil	Yellow, white, orange, pink
Erythronium (Japanese pagoda)	Yellow, white, pink
Fritillaria imperialis	Red, orange, yellow
Fritillaria meleagris	Purple and white, white
Fritillaria michailovskyi	Bronze, yellow
Hyacinth, Dutch	Pink, purple, blue, red, rose white, yellow, apricot
Ipheion	White, blue
Leucojum (Snowflake)	White
Muscari (Grape hyacinth)	Deep blue, light blue, white
Ornithogalum umbellatum	White, pale green
Puschkinia (Lebanon squill)	Pale blue
Scilla hispanica (Spanish bluebells)	White, blue, pink.
Scilla siberica (Squill)	Bright, electric blue, pale blue, white
Tulip, Mayflowering	All colors

THE COMBINATIONS ARE ENDLESS: STANDARD DWARF IRISES 'CHUBBY CHEEKS' WITH ANEMONES (ABOVE) AND MINIATURE DWARF IRISES 'GENTLE GRACE' IN THE SPRING.

MAY-BLOOMING PERENNIALS AS IRIS COMPANIONS

Many perennials bloom in May and are suitable for combining with May-flowering irises.

PLANT	DESCRIPTION
Achillea (Yarrow)	Sulfur yellow, pale yellow, rose, white, lavender
Anthemis (Golden marguerite)	Bright yellow; daisy-shaped
Aquilegia (Columbine)	All colors
Arenaria (Sandwort)	Mats of white
Centaurea montana (Cornflower)	Deep blue
Dianthus (Pinks)	Many shades of red, pink, salmon, white
Dicentra (Bleeding heart)	Pink, white
Geranium (Cranesbill)	Blue, pink, magenta, white
Geum	Orange, yellow, crimson, pink
Heuchera (Coral bells)	Pink, red, white
Myosotis (Forget-me-not)	Tiny blue blossoms
Peony	Red, pink, yellow, white
Phlox divaricata (Wild phlox)	Blues
Phlox stolonifera (Creeping phlox)	Blue, red, pink, white
Phlox subulata (Moss pinks)	Blue, red, pink, white
Polemonium (Jacob's Ladder)	Blue
Polygonatum (Solomon's Seal)	Creamy white
Saponaria (Soapwort)	Pink mats
Trollius (Globeflower)	Bright yellow
Veronica prostrata (Speedwell)	Blue mats

ABOVE: THIS IMPRESSIVE SHOW OF TALL BEARDED IRISES AT MT. CONGREVE IN WATERFORD COUNTY, IRELAND, IS SOMETHING NEITHER YOU NOR I WOULD PROBABLY BE ABLE TO ACCOMPLISH. BUT THIS DISPLAY CAN BE CONVERTED TO A MORE MODEST SCALE. NOTICE HOW THE IRISES ARE PLANTED IN BLOCKS OF COLOR, ALTERNATING DARK WITH LIGHT. BELOW: IRISES WITH PEONIES AND *ALLIUMS*.

COMPLEMENTING SIBERIAN IRISES

PLANT	DESCRIPTION
Alchemilla mollis	Lime-green foliage; yellow blossoms front
Astilbe	White flowering varieties
Clematis 'Mr. President'	Deep purple
Dicentra spectabilis 'Alba'	White
Geranium sanguineum 'Brookside'	Pink
Heuchera	Pink
Hosta fortunei 'Marginato-alba'	Green and white foliage
Mertensia virginica (Virginia bluebells)	Sky-blue bell-shaped blossoms
Oriental poppy	Salmon varieties
Salvia 'Blue Hill'	Brilliant blue
Annual Silene	Pink, white, very deep purple-pink

OUTDOOR CONTAINERS

Bulbous irises in containers add lovely dimensions to any garden. Use them to grace your front entryway or line your walks. Or place them on decks and terraces for a spring show, so that you can sit and enjoy them on balmy days. They are also perfect accents for courtyards, balconies, flat rooftops, driveways, window ledges, fire escapes, and retaining walls. Use them for camouflaging unattractive storage sheds or garbage cans. Some gardeners prefer a unified look: one type or color of flower, such as sunny yellow I. *danfordiae* irises in a small, terra-cotta bulb pan. Others prefer to mix the blue and purple colors of I. *reticulata* with the yellow *danfordiae*. You can add early-spring-blooming pansies to the pots once they have begun to bloom.

AT THE EDGE OF A WOODLAND GARDEN STANDARD DWARF BEARDED IRISES, *AJUGA*, HOSTA, *DAPHNE* 'CAROL MACKIE,' AND CAMMASIA ARE ALL IN BLOOM.

Start by planting your containers as instructed for forcing. Then put containers outdoors in a place sheltered from the wind, extreme cold (in the North), and hot sun (in the South). Outdoor containers should be a minimum of 14 inches across to withstand overwintering outdoors. In extreme cold climates, put containers in an unheated, protected area like a garage or shed. If they are too heavy to move, wrap containers with newspaper and burlap. In the South, keep pots cool, positioned out of the sun, preferably with a northern exposure. And avoid dark containers, which trap heat.

Water the containers over the winter. Aside from being essential for growing, water also protects the bulbs from frost injury. Keep the soil moist, but not soggy. Mulch will help retain moisture.

With containers planted and positioned for the winter, and fall planting directly in the ground all behind you, you can sit back and wait for spring, knowing that your garden will be more beautiful than ever before.

SIBERIAN IRISES AND LADY'S MANTLE SURROUND THE POND AT OLD WESTBURY GARDENS IN NEW YORK. OPPOSITE: THE GOLD OF THE TALL BEARDED IRIS AND THE YELLOW OF THE RIBBON GRASS AND THE *HOSTA* COME TOGETHER HARMONIOUSLY.

5 Irises Indoors

A few easy steps will ensure that your flower arrangements will be as beautiful and long-lasting as possible.

CUTTING IRISES

Cutting and conditioning most irises for indoor arrangements is very straightforward. In all cases—except for Spurias and Louisianas—cut when the first bud opens on a stem. (Cut Spurias and Louisianas when they start showing color at the end of the first bud.) Place cuttings in cool water as soon as possible. As each flower spends itself, pinch it off. Some arrangers suggest putting one teaspoon of sugar in the vase water, but most do not; it most assuredly will not hurt the flowers if you do.

Selecting Irises for Arrangements

Bulbous Dutch irises have the longest vase life of all and are thus the choice of many professionals for flower arrangements.

Median, and Miniature Dwarf Bearded irises are ideal for mixing with other varieties. They last about a week.

Spurias are also great cut flowers, having some of the showiest blooms. They mix well with other types of flowers and have interesting flower shapes for arrangements. They last about a week.

Louisiana irises are among the most beautiful of all flowers in arrangements. Cut stems about two inches above the ground when the first bud shows color. Each stalk bears from five to seven buds and often two or more are open at the same time. Behind each flower there is usually a second bud, which will open later. Blooms last about a week.

Japanese irises, although very flamboyant, last for only one day in an arrangement and then flop over, so unless you are looking for a very short-lived arrangement, select from other varieties. One Japanese tradition is to bring them inside to watch each bud open and close over a period of several days.

For the longest-lasting cut irises, change the water every two days and keep the flowers out of sunlight.

Tall Bearded irises, although very beautiful, are difficult to mix with other flowers, and often require very large vases to make them attractive.

To Make Your Arrangements Last Longer

Use plain, cool water.

Change the water every two days—don't just top it off. This is the single most important thing you can do to keep your flowers looking fresh.

Keep flowers out of direct sunlight, and move them to a cool place at night.

Do not mix irises with daffodils, since daffodil stems give off a compound that is toxic to other flowers.

Keep cut flowers away from fruit, which releases a gas that causes flowers to age more quickly.

FORCING BULBOUS IRISES

Although none of the Bearded or Beardless irises lend themselves to forcing, the small Bulbous irises I. *danfordiae* and I. *reticulata* do force quite well. With a little bit of effort you can have your house filled with delicate blossoms and a lovely violet-like scent during the bleak midwinter months. Here's how you do it.

Selecting Containers

Although you can grow Bulbous irises in just about any kind of container imaginable, the traditional clay or plastic "bulb pans" are probably the best because of their essential drainage holes. As a rule, the pot should be about twice as deep as the height of a bulb. In other words, an *Iris reticulata* or I. *danfordiae* bulb that measures 1 1/2 –2 inches from top to bottom should be potted in a 4-inch-deep pot.

Conditioning Containers

Some containers have to be conditioned before planting. Soak new terra-cotta or clay containers in water overnight so that they will not absorb the water necessary for the planting medium. Soak used terra-cotta, clay, or plastic containers overnight in a solution of one part household bleach to three parts water to kill any disease organism that might be on the surface of the container. New plastic containers need no conditioning.

Soil Mixture

Use a soil mixture such as Redi-Earth or Terra-lite that is recommended for starting seedlings. Potting soil is not good, as it is usually too heavy. If you wish to make your own soil mix, combine equal amounts of packaged potting soil, sphagnum peat moss (wet and then squeezed almost dry), and horticultural or builder's sand. Add 1 cup perlite or horticultural vermiculite to each quart of soil mix.

Planting

First, cover the drainage holes in the bottoms of the pots with pebbles, rocks, broken flowerpot shards, or the white plastic "popcorn" used by mail-order houses to ship merchandise. Then fill the pot about two-thirds full with soil mix. Set a bulb so its top is half an inch below the rim of the pot. Adjust the soil level if necessary. Set more bulbs on the soil, making sure they do not touch. Fill the pot with soil mix. Do not pack it down; bulb roots require loosely packed soil to grow properly.

Water the pots thoroughly. Fill in cavities with more soil mix if necessary. Be sure to label each pot, so that when it comes time to force bloom you will know which is which.

The Chilling Process

In order to bring Bulbous irises to bloom before their normal time, you must provide a cool environment. There are three different ways to do this.

First, you can sink pots into a cold frame outdoors and then cover them with a 6–8-inch layer of salt hay or sand. This isn't the most convenient method, since you'll have to make trips out to the garden in the dead of winter to see if the shoots are emerging, and in very cold weather, it is often difficult to remove the protective covering because it is frozen stiff or covered with ice and snow. However, if you have no other option, this is the way to do it.

The second way, which is much easier and equally as effective, is to place the pots in a cold cellar or an unheated garage. The temperature ideally should stay between 30 and 50° F. Cover them with newspaper so that no light falls on the bulbs. In general, the pots will need to be watered approximately every four weeks. Even so, it is a good idea to check the soil every week; if it is dry to the touch, water moderately. Good root growth is essential for successful forcing.

The third method is to chill the bulbs in a refrigerator. Place the

93

potted bulbs inside and check every now and then to see if watering is necessary. Never place pots in the freezer.

Forcing Bloom

After the cooling period, which ends when shoots have emerged and are about 2 to 3 inches high, it is time to bring the pots into warmer temperatures to begin the forcing process. The shoots will be a light yellow-green color. Place the pots in a 50–60° F indoor location, either in darkness or in bright, indirect sunlight, for three to five weeks. During this period, bulbs will develop strong top growth. Check soil occasionally, and water if necessary.

As soon as flower buds appear, place pots in a location with cool temperatures (50–60° F) and direct sunlight. Eight to ten days later, once the buds begin to show color, it's time to force bloom; move the pots to wherever they will be admired. Keep in mind that the cooler the temperatures, especially at night; the longer the bulbs will stay in bloom. Under optimum conditions, plants displayed in an area no warmer than 65° F should stay in bloom for a week to ten days.

When they are finished blooming, throw *Iris danfordiae* out, because they rarely bloom a second year, even when planted outdoors. *Iris reticulata* may bloom again, so clean and dry bulbs and plant them outdoors in soil in the fall. However, to be sure of success, buy new bulbs; they are quite inexpensive.

Timing

If you want to have bulbs in bloom on a particular date—Easter, for example—keep in mind that rooting takes eight to ten weeks at approximately 30–50° F in a dark location. Forcing takes approximately eight to ten days in a cool 50–60° F location in bright, indirect light. So the total time from planting to flowering is nine to eleven weeks.

SOURCES

VISIT THESE websites and order catalogues from the following nurseries. The websites and catalogues include many glorious color photographs, as well as growing information, which will help you make your selections.

BEARDED AND BEARDLESS IRISES

DRAYCOTT GARDENS
16815 Falls Road
Upperco, MD 21155
(410) 374-4788
www.GardenEureka.com/DRAYC

FIELDSTONE GARDENS
620 Quaker Lane
Vassalboro, ME 04989-9713
(207) 923-3836
www.fieldstonegardens.com

GORMLEY GREENERY
6717 Martha Drive
Cedar Hill, MO 63016
(636) 274-7435
www.flash.net/~mindpath/
gormley/

IRIS CITY GARDENS
7675 Younger Creek Road
Primm Springs, TN 38476
(800) 934-IRIS (4747)
www.iriscitygardens.com

McMILLEN'S IRIS GARDEN
R.R.#1
Norwich, Ontario N0J 1P0
Canada
(519) 468-6508
www.execulink.com/~iris/

SCHREINER'S IRIS GARDENS
3625 Quinaby Road NE
Salem, Oregon 97303
(800) 525-2367
www.schreinersgardens.com

WHITE FLOWER FARM
P.O. Box 50
Litchfield, CT 06759-0050
(800) 503-9624
www.whiteflowerfarm.com

BULBOUS IRISES

BRENT AND BECKY'S BULBS
7463 Heath Trail
Gloucester, VA 23061
(877) 661-2852
www.brentandbeckysbulbs.com

McCLURE & ZIMMERMAN
108 W. Winnebago St.
P.O. Box 368
Friesland WI 53935-0368
(800) 883-6998
www.mzbulb.com

JOHN SCHEEPERS
23 Tulip Drive
Bantam, CT 06750-1631
(860) 567-0838
www.johnscheepers.com

VAN BOURGONDIEN
245 Route 109
P.O. Box 1000
Babylon, NY 11702-9004
(800) 622-9997
www.dutchbulbs.com

FOR MORE INFORMATION ABOUT IRISES: THE AMERICAN IRIS SOCIETY AND LOCAL AIS-AFFILIATED GROUPS ARE TREMENDOUS SOURCES OF INFORMATION. CONTACT THE SOCIETY THROUGH THEIR VERY GOOD WEBSITE (WWW.IRISES.ORG) FOR DETAILS.

INDEX

Page numbers in italics refer to illustrations